THE
Old Photographs
SERIES

BARLBOROUGH,
CLOWNE, CRESWELL
AND WHITWELL

A local photographer about to say 'Watch the birdie'.

THE
Old Photographs
SERIES

BARLBOROUGH, CLOWNE, CRESWELL AND WHITWELL

Compiled by
L.T. Yaw

CHALFORD

BATH • AUGUSTA • RENNES

First published 1994
Copyright © L.T. Yaw, 1994

The Chalford Publishing Company Limited
St Mary's Mill, Chalford, Stroud
Gloucestershire GL6 8NX

ISBN 0 7524 031 2

Typesetting and origination by
Alan Sutton Limited
Printed in Great Britain by
Redwood Books, Trowbridge

Contents

A 1791 map of N. E. Derbyshire showing the villages of Barlborough, Clowne, Creswell and Whitwell. The Dukes of Leeds, Newcastle, Norfolk, Portland and Rutland, as well as the Rodes family, all held land in this area.

Introduction

Throughout the ages Barlborough, Clowne, Creswell with Elmton and Whitwell have figured prominently in our national history. Their central inland position, in close proximity to the North/South and East/West trade routes, is the main reason for this prominence.

Before history was recorded, the caves in Creswell Crags gave shelter to the hunter gatherers on their annual migration through Central Europe, when Britain was still an integral part of the continent. Pin Hole Cave provided Britain's earliest example of art, attributed to the Old Stone Age more than 10,000 BC and given the name of Creswellian culture, while the workings in the stone quarry at Whitwell during the last decade have revealed burial chambers associated with the New Stone Age of about 1800 BC.

In recorded history the Anglo-Saxon Chronicle shows that Whitwell was on the border from Dore (Sheffield) to the River Humber estuary, separating the large kingdoms of Mercia and Northumbria; many warring factions would certainly pass this way. The Domesday Survey also lists the four settlements: Barlborough (Barleburgh) and Whitwell (Whitewell) are recorded in a single entry as a manor and berewick held by Ralph Fitzhubert as tenant-in-chief; Clowne (Clune) was held by Ernui under the king with two ox-gangs of land belonging to the manor of Whitwell; in Elmton (Helmetune) there was a priest, thirty six villeins and two borders.

Two centuries of comparative calm after the Norman invasion saw the institution of the manorial system. Sir John Manners established himself in the Old Hall at Whitwell. The alleged elopement between John Manners and Dorothy Vernon in 1558 provides the best-known story about Haddon Hall, Derbyshire. The Longford family held part of the manor of Barlborough and the Pole family resided at Park Hall but it was Judge Francis Rodes who began purchasing land around Barlborough and built Barlborough Hall between 1582 and 1584. Judge Rodes also held Elmton which in later years was sold to the Duke of Portland. There is some evidence that the Mennill family were the lords of Clowne manor until it became associated with Bolsover Castle and then passed to the Portlands at Welbeck. The Frechevilles held the manor at Steetley which was eventually joined with Whitwell.

Following the outbreak of the Civil War a skirmish took place on Whitwell Common, when Royalist forces advancing from Welbeck Abbey clashed with Parliamentarians commanded by Rodes of Barlborough. A local man, John Battersby, had one hand cut off by a sword in the fray; one of his ancestors is featured in this book.

Welbeck came into the possession of the Cavendish family when the Second Duke of Portland married the granddaughter of the Duke of Newcastle. Thereafter they were great benefactors of the local villages, providing finance for schools and hospitals, opportunities for employment on the vast estates and becoming patrons of the Anglican churches. Each village has a Norman church, while the one at Steetley is reported to be the finest example of its style in Europe. Both Methodist and Roman Catholic churches are prominent, and the Salvation Army is firmly established in Clowne.

The passing of the Local Government Act in 1894 led to each village electing a Parish Council to take over the civil functions of the Vestry meetings. Representatives from the four Parish Councils were then elected to serve on the Clowne Rural District Council which governed the area effectively until authority was eventually transferred to the Bolsover District Council.

Having followed an agricultural economy into the nineteenth century, the effects of the Industrial Revolution held sway and the landowners allowed the development of the coalfield to progress with at least one colliery being opened in each of the villages. Unfortunately, after one hundred years of working, the colliery closure programme has brought this extensive activity to an end. The mines which once scarred the landscape with their spoil heaps are now scarring the hearts of the miners following their closure.

The collieries were keen promoters of sport — football, cricket, bowls, tennis and indoor games. There was a popular Derbyshire saying that when the County Cricket Club required a fast bowler, they only had to call down the pit shaft; the achievements of Les Jackson for both county and country are ample proof of this, while Mr G.G. Walker, Whitwell, played for the Gentlemen of England and Derbyshire. Joe Davis, former World Billiards and Snooker Champion was born in Whitwell and Mr A. Marshall, Clowne was the one-arm Billiards Champion of Great Britain. The four villages have certainly produced their quota of players proficient in all fields of sport and are continuing to do so. Inter-village rivalry has been keen over the years, yet invariably friendly with an interchange of participants as families move between the villages.

But what of the future? Life in Barlborough, Clowne, Creswell and Whitwell since the accession of Queen Victoria to the throne in 1837 is portrayed by the pictures in this book. Each village is unique in its social, economic and religious activities, yet each joins with the others, when appropriate, to form a generic community. The reader can reflect upon one hundred and fifty years since the camera was invented — but what will be the prominent themes of the next book of Old Photographs? Computers! Electronics! Robots! Or will life return to the old cottage industries?

One
Barlborough

Barlborough Colliery (Oxcroft No 3). Situated off Boughton Lane, Clowne, the site was cleared in the 1950s although a few colliery houses still remain.

The Village Cross, with its unusual sundial, is thought to have stood in the same place since Norman times.

Barlborough village with the familiar water tower on the skyline. The storage tanks used to receive water from an underground supply beneath Manton Colliery but have since been demolished.

10

A country cottage on Park Street with thatched roof, leaded windows and a well-stocked garden, built in the late 1700s.

A Barlborough cottage decorated as a welcome to the soldiers returning from the Crimean War.

The original Dusty Miller. The new inn stands adjacent to the cottages.

Street decoration for the wedding of Felicity Locker-Lampson in 1928. Clarke's cobblers shop (now demolished) stands on the right.

Barlborough East End with a loan pedestrian and a solitary vehicle on the crossroads. No need for the roundabout which accepts traffic from the busy M1 motorway nowadays.

The De Rhodes crossroads before the roundabout was constructed.

The last filling station before the M1 motorway. Owner of the garage and one time official at Peggler's Pit, Mr Bunting, is in the foreground with his son 'Emick' on the left.

The opening ceremony for the Barlborough
Primitive Methodist Chapel in 1913.

Barlborough School appropriately decorated for the coronation of Queen Elizabeth II in 1953.
Mr Rex Atkin, headmaster, is standing in the playground.

The Rev Griffiths, a former Rector of Barlborough c. 1914, with his wife.

The Alms Houses erected as a hospital in 1752 by Margaret and Mary Pole and endowed for six widows and spinsters, who were to receive a weekly allowance and coal annually.

Arthur Lowe ponders beneath the arch of the Boaler family memorial at Sycamore House. Joseph Boaler died on 14 January 1833 and his wife Marta on 17 July 1832. Their remains were deposited at Carburton in the County of Nottingham.

Barlborough Church. The only remaining Norman part of this ancient church built c. 1170 is the fine arcade. The lower part of the Tower and the Chancel Arch are both Early English, while the Tower Arch is a good example of a five-pointed Gothic arch.

A concert party performing around 1910.

The wedding group after the marriage of John Parr to Winnie Archer *c.* 1910.

Some Barlborough members of the Druids. On the back row, Mr Herbert Wheat is second left and Mr A. Lowe fourth left.

An outing to Sherwood Forest. The group are posing beneath the Major Oak with Sarah Anne Lowe and Eliza Parr right of centre in the middle row.

Lord Grey de Ruthyn. Said to have been Britain's poorest peer, he was Guardian of the Canine Society of Great Britain and popular with the local residents.

Two

Clowne

Clowne Southgate Colliery seen from Station Hill. A serious fire, which destroyed No. 1 engine house on 18 March 1920, threatened the mine itself but a rescue lasting six hours released all who were underground. The end came on 17 January 1929 when the mine flooded and was never opened again — two pit ponies were the only fatalities on this occasion.

Southgate Colliery began life in 1875 when Miss Bowden of Southgate House cut the first sod. Production started two years later and the first fatality was Rufus Mew in 1878. Twelve men were involved in a cage accident on 22 November 1911 when three men were killed named Bunday, Marlow and Wild.

BUMPMILL POND CLOWNE

Bumpmill Pond was used for treating flax in the making of 'bumph' cloth, hence the derivation of the name. Three young people died here on 25 January 1888: Jim Draper and Sam Hibbard were teaching Carrye Rounds to skate when the ice broke.

Holly Cottages overlooking Mill Yard with an entrance from Mill Street.

The royal visit of King George V and Queen Mary in 1914. The children on the platform were suitably dressed and arranged in the form of the Union Jack.

A troop of soldiers marching to the docks for overseas duty in 1914. A member of the Upton family is in the troop.

Members of the Wesleyan Chapel before embarking on an outing to Skegness.

Clowne Army Cadets with their Commanding Officer, 'Billy' Holmes, seated in the centre of the second row.

Clowne War Memorial and the Green during the First World War peace celebrations.

Church Street with the Norman church almost one mile from the village centre. One explanation is that the building stands close to an ancient ridgeway and was once the site of a monastery.

The United Methodist Free Church was established in Clowne in the mid-1800s. The original site was sold to a railway company for £1,200 in 1894 and the foundation stone for the new building, costing £2,000, was laid by T. D. Bolton, MP in the same year.

The shortage of swimming trunks was no deterrent for these youngsters relaxing by a pool in Clowne Grips.

This Victorian corn mill, standing in the centre of the village, produced flour for local consumption.

The original Angel Hotel at the junction of Mansfield Road with High Street. This is one of the four inns listed in Bagshaw's Directory, 1846, when the innkeeper was William Jepson.

North Road, Clowne before the advent of the motor car.

Hardware store at the junction of North Road with Station Road. Vacuum oil is advertised but not a motor car in sight, fortunately for the infant riding in the middle of the road. The premises later became a grocer's shop with post office.

Cottages at the bottom of Creswell Road adjacent to Nelme's Bakery. Flooding was caused when Arnold Sibring lifted the sluice to lower the water level in Bumpmill Pond then could not replace it.

The two railway stations built by the Midland and the Lancashire and East Coast Railway Companies. The Midland Station at 'Clown' was renamed Clown & Barlborough on 4 July 1938, with the letter 'e' added to Clown on 18 June 1951.

The Edwards family with thirteen children. Homes were small and crowded; the children would sleep head to toe in shared beds with a curtain to partition the bedroom.

Clowne Picture House. The Palace stood adjacent to the old school buildings, now part of the Tertiary College.

The cottage of Ernest Briggs with pantile roof, sashcord windows and iron gates. Iron gates like these were generally commandeered for wartime munitions.

An early twentieth century wedding group outside the Co-operative Society premises on High Street.

F. J. Edwards, High Street merchant. The business was taken over by Bowskills.

A. Hibbard's well-stocked butcher's shop in 1910 showing little concern for the food hygiene demanded nowadays.

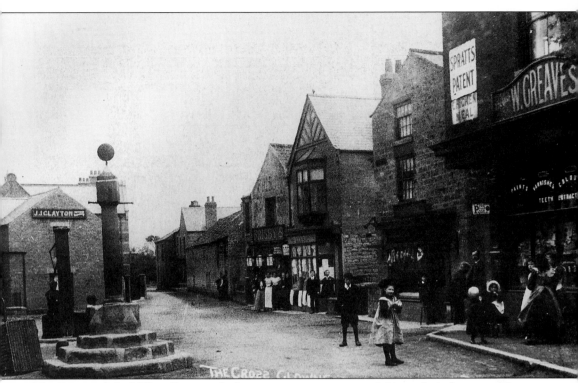

The Cross and the Village Pump with the surviving stone stump of the stocks in between. Note the invitation to have teeth extracted at W. Greaves hardware store.

Southgate House. The family seat of the Bowden family traceable back to Henry Bowden, who died in 1665. The house was sold by Lt-Col. W. Butler-Bowden, DSO together with twenty-three other Lots, including farms, cottages, smallholdings and building land. During the Second World War the house was requisitioned, first as an army camp and later as a prisoner-of-war camp. The house is now used as an hotel with a garden centre alongside.

Three
Creswell

Creswell Colliery, sunk in 1894-96. This was the scene of a tragic disaster on 26 September 1950, when an underground fire claimed the lives of eighty miners.

An early print of Creswell Crags showing the mill cottages at the southern entrance to the limestone gorge.

The Star Inn. The inn stood at the southern entrance to the Crags; David Green was the last landlord at the turn of the century.

The Rev. Charles Stanley Branson and the church choir outside Elmton Church in 1946.

The Rev. Ken Servante with the choir and congregation of Elmton Church for the dedication of the Lych Gate in 1971.

Elmton Church, but not the original one mentioned in Domesday Book. Rebuilding of the present church began in 1771: provision of a tower had been intended since the tower walls are five feet thick. However, the peal of three bells, cast in 1845, are housed in the turret.

Members of St Mary Magdalene Church form the cast for a Nativity Play c. 1920. Rear: Henry Hardwick, Jack Marples, J.G. Linneker, Robinson, Tom Starkey. Front: Joe Warren, Elsie Hunt, Mrs Paget. Children: Fretwell, Elsie Faulkener, Margery Till.

The Primitive Methodist Church. Built by the Bolsover Colliery Company *c.* 1908, at a cost of £1,400, the building seated 280 persons.

The Wesleyan Church, built at a cost of £1,100.

A 'coach and pair' at the turn of the century. The horses were stabled behind Botham's Row: white horses were used for weddings and black horses for carting coal.

A proud Victorian wedding group. The Holmes and Freeman families gathered outside the home of the newly married couple on Baker Street.

Creswell children embark on an outing by horse and waggon to Welbeck in June 1914, despite the inclement weather.

Hospital Sunday. The procession passes along Church Street c. 1910 with Waller's shop on the corner and St Mary Magdalene's Church in the distance before the addition of side aisles and tower.

Portland Corner, Creswell.

The Portland Hotel corner in 1909. The single-storey building in the foreground was erected in 1897 and was used as a Roman Catholic Church, a mortuary, a gamesroom and as headquarters for the local branch of the Debyshire Miners' Union.

The old mill and pond in the ancient fort of Markland Grips c. 1905.

A procession passing by the old Portland Hotel in 1910. The new Portland Hotel opened on 24 December 1938.

Street gatherings were a natural way of socialising one hundred years ago. Here a group of Creswell villagers are enjoying a game of marbles called 'Killer'.

The Electric Palace. Opened on King Street *c*. 1910, the building was burned down on 29 July 1938, being replaced by the Regors Cinema in 1939.

Children standing outside the old cinema on King Street *c*. 1928.

Creswell Trombone Quartet. Winners of the World Championship in 1945 with Conductor Harold Moss, they were Maurice Teasdale, Bernard Bramley, Harold Patterson and Tommy Oughton.

The Creswell Colliery Band 1926. The band with their Conductor David Aspinall display the Belle Vue and Newcastle Championship trophies which they won the previous year.

Knowles and Wildgoose butcher's shop at 12 Sheffield Road before the First World War. Mr Knowles was taken prisoner-of-war in 1914.

Botham's Row on Main Street *c.* 1910, now known as Sheffield Road.

The soup kitchen during the miners' strike of 1926 with Mrs Hayes and Messrs Saul, Vardy, Fall and Curris among the helpers.

A group of fitters/blacksmith/painter at Creswell Colliery *c*. 1955. Standing: Bill Heath, Nev Dawes, Dennis Jone, Bill Asher. Middle: Jim Sleigh, Harry Lockwood, Jack Fletcher, Jack Brown. Front: Alec Leyland, George Heath, Bill Woodhead.

'Dan' Storer, who was totally blind, out on his round selling yeast.

Reg. Barlow, fruiterer, clearing the snow from around his dray in 1947. The loss of one leg seemed to be no impediment and he was reputed to have been 'as strong as an ox'.

Workers surfacing the new road to Creswell Colliery *c.* 1940. The lady is Mrs Doris Clarke who reached the age of ninety-two in 1994.

Creswell schoolchildren wearing suitable labels as they gather outside the Institute before embarking on an outing *c.* 1930.

A cricket team comprising members of the Slater family. One player appeared for Derbyshire CCC in 1904 and another in 1930, while a third played football with Sheffield Wednesday.

Creswell C of E School XI, 1923. Winners of the East Derbyshire League and Teachers Charity Cup. Standing left to right: D. Ford, H. Voce, A. Stubbings, E. Vardy, F. Sargent, W. Oliver, E. Coalwood, G. Hardwick. Seated: W. Bird, W. Williams, G. Wood, R. Edwards, S. Ford.

Four

Whitwell

Whitwell Colliery with the Little Scotland cottages on Belph Common c. 1895.

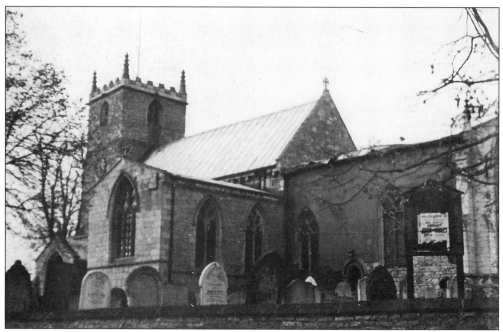

Whitwell Parish Church before the chancel roof was raised. The graves were later removed for the road widening scheme.

The Old Hall. The Elizabethan home of Sir John Manners became a private school in the nineteenth century and was later used as a church hall before being restored as a private residence.

The Rev. Canon Mason, Rector of
Whitwell 1874-1908, with his sister at the
entrance to the Old Rectory.

Robert Ellis — 'The Gaffer'. Headmaster of
Whitwell School 1890-1926 and church
organist/choirmaster for twenty-five years,
he died in 1950.

Pear Tree Cottage in Whitwell Square. The building was demolished in 1923 to make way for the War Memorial.

The stone from Pear Tree Cottage was bought by Mr Tom Mottishaw who rebuilt the cottage in Hodthorpe in 1924 — the only stone cottage in the village.

Whitwell War Memorial. Unveiled by His Grace, The Duke of Portland, KG and dedicated by the Lord Bishop of Southwell on Saturday, 26 April 1924.

The Duke of Portland's words at the unveiling ceremony were prophetic, 'This monument will be buffeted by the winds, beaten by the rain'. Archdeacon Crosse surveys the damage. The memorial was several inches shorter when rebuilt in 1927.

The interior of the Star Tea Company premises before the fire.

Damage after the fire at the Star Tea Company premises at the corner of Coronation Street with Larpit Lane (Welbeck Street) in 1904.

Whitwell's own Coronation Street *c*. 1910. The Star Tea Company stood on the right-hand corner of the road junction.

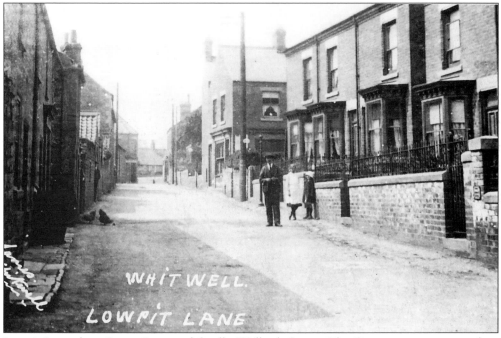

Lowpit Lane, later Larpit Lane and finally Welbeck Street. The Co-operative premises (top left) were later transferred to the opposite side of Spring Hill.

The west end of Whitwell from the allotments on the High Hill, showing the Church, the Old Rectory, the Dicken, Tea Pot Yard, Long Curtain Row, the Old Hall and Manor House Farms.

The Dicken from Stoney Hill, formerly Godley Hill and Palmer's Hill. The cottage on the right was a blacksmith's forge in 1860.

The George Inn, High Street. A staging post for the Gainsborough to Chesterfield stagecoach; the mounting steps are visible at the corner of the building.

The Chesterfield to Worksop turnpike road crosses The Green. Mr Lindley's Harness and Saddlers shop is on the left.

The Empire Day celebrations 1904. The lady in the carriage is probably Her Grace, The Duchess of Portland.

Celebration parade for the Coronation of King George V, 1911, marching past Pear Tree Cottage.

St Lawrence Feast Sunday. The service on the High Hill, by tradition, was never before 4 August and never after 10 August. Long Curtain Row is in the background.

High Hill Quarry before the building of St Lawrence View and Jubilee Gardens in the 1930s.

General view of Whitwell showing the development after the sinking of the colliery in 1890. The Schools, Miner's Welfare, Colliery Row and Minkley's Brewery chimney are all visible.

High Street with Thomas Rotherham's Post Office on the left. The walled frontage to the Boot and Shoe Inn and Pear Tree Cottage are visible in the background.

Whitwell Square. The village pump on the left supplied water to the village, the Town Well was used for watering the horses, with Pear Tree Cottage behind and the Boot and Shoe Inn in the background.

The Yeoman's Cottage. Built in the sixteenth century and situated to the rear of Birk's Farm, the building was demolished in 1983.

The Reading Room. Provided by Canon Mason in 1877: on Thursdays for the 'Soldiers of Christ'; on Saturdays for all men and boys — no boy under fifteen years was admitted unless confirmed. The Guardians were duty bound to report any misconduct or bad language to the Rector.

The Whitwell Kinema later known as the Ritz. Built with brown and white glazed bricks the cinema stood on Station Road opposite to the Social Club.

Part of three cottages opposite Hodthorpe School, which were demolished *c*. 1936 to make way for three new dwellings one being occupied by the village policeman, Pc Knapp.

The Beer Off, Steetley. The premises were at the end of the Ten Row near the entrance to Steetley Quarry; Robert Sibbring and his family are standing at the gate.

The Old Mill. Built on Mill Lane in 1829, the mill is shown undergoing maintenance *c*. 1890. This well-known landmark was demolished in 1962 to make way for housing development.

The Half Moon Inn. Situated on the Chesterfield to Worksop turnpike road at Red Hill and built in the 1700s, the premises have subsequently undergone many changes. Note the BP gear-type petrol pump.

Five

Schooldays

Empire Day celebrations outside St Lawrence Public Elementary School, Whitwell *c*. 1912.

Barlborough Hall. Built *c.* 1584 for Sir Francis Rodes, this stately home became a Roman Catholic preparatory school in 1928.

Whitwell Mixed County School gardens in 1937, situated in front of the Old Rectory.

Staveley Netherthorpe Grammar School cricket team in 1939. Players from all four villages included P. Bantam, P. Gallagher, Ken Calow, Ken Atkin, Ian Medlam, Albert Yates, Robert Brain and Les Yaw.

The five-member School Board opened a new Clowne school in 1877 for 250 girls and 250 infants at a cost of £2,250. Twelve years later a Board School for 250 boys was built at a cost of £2,000.

Clowne Junior schoolchildren *c.* 1910.

Barlborough Girls Friendly Society perform 'Madam Muddles Dream' in 1931.

A group of Barlborough children on holiday at the seaside in 1931.

Hodthorpe Elementary Mixed School 1920. Cyril (Squib) Beardsley is second from left and cousin Lucy eight from left on the back row; brother Jim is in the centre of the front row.

Hodthorpe School. Pupils enjoying tea in the Big Room, with Reg Cooper, Derek Wordley and Sam Cottam in the foreground.

St Lawrence Football Club. Football and cricket clubs were organised through the church during Canon Mason's time (1874-1908); Mr Carter is prominent in the bowler hat.

Whitwell Church of England Infants School *c.* 1911. Miss Dorothy Vickers (Mrs Streets) is seated front right with Miss Maiden next to her.

Miss Lambert and Miss Glover forsake Clowne for a cautious paddle at the seaside *c.* 1910.

Junior members of the Girls' Friendly Society with their leaders at Clowne *c.* 1920.

The lads of Skinback Row, Spring Hill, Whitwell. The rabbit trader used to sell rabbits here for twopence each provided he could have the skins back.

Creswell Infants' School. Miss Lancashire, Miss Stacey, Miss Woodward and Miss Cocking outside the school, which is decorated for the Silver Jubilee celebrations in 1935.

Creswell Senior School. Children at play in the school yard before the First World War with the old Portland Arms public house in the background.

A group of Creswell schoolchildren with their teachers *c.* 1924.

Six

On the Farm

A three-horse digger plough tilling the soil on Red Hill adjacent to the Chesterfield to Worksop turnpike road c. 1920.

W. Locke pauses with his plough team.

Mr Bellimore seated on his reaping machine *c.* 1898.

Mr Brown with a combine harvester before 1939.

Mr W. Locke with his two-horse plough. He later became landlord of the Traveller's Rest Inn on Creswell Road.

The threshing machine at work with a team of six to eight men. The men in the foreground used to carry sacks of grain weighing eighteen stones to the granary, sometimes up a ladder.

The oat straw being cleared from the chaffing machine for later use as feed for the cattle and horses.

Haymaking. The farmer's boy leads the horse with the commands of 'Whoah' and ' Owd Ya'.

The shepherd leads his flock along Station Road, Whitwell; his dog will be driving the sheep from the rear.

(Left): Mr George Warrener Jnr with his son George Anthony outside Hickenwood Farm in 1939.

Drabble's Farm. Situated between Whitwell and Creswell, the farm was later demolished to make way for the Steetley Quarry.

Victor Widdowson, Clowne, ready for the harvest field with his double-barrel gun.

Warrener's Farm from the High Hill, Bakestone Moor showing how the homestead farms were located within the village. In later years farm buildings were erected within their particular field complex.

John Blagg's steam engine involved in the Silver Jubilee celebrations of 1977. Similar engines were used to drive the threshing machine and for pulling the ploughshare from one headland to the other.

A mixed group *c.* 1910 equipped with axes and cross-cut saws ready for timber felling.

The Mill Farm complex in Markland Grips.

A combine harvester typical of the 1930s.

The last load of hay approaches the Butcher's Arms, en route to a homestead farm in Whitwell.

Mellor's threshing machine outside the Rose and Crown Inn, Creswell *c.* 1898.

Seven

On the Move

Creswell Road with Clowne Southgate Colliery on the left.

Tom Smith, Clowne, with his fixed-wheel racing cycle — no mudguards, no rear brake and an uncomfortable-looking saddle.

FIRE ENGINE WITH TEA AND COFFEE URNS
CONNECTED TO BOILING ENGINE.

Raised by the sixth Duke of Portland and maintained by Welbeck Estate, the fire engine was occasionally summoned to the local villages.

The motor cycle combination carries two visitors to the local photographer, Mr Hammond *c.* 1920.

Whitwell Motor-cycle & Light Car Club 1925. Bill Phillips is sixth from the left wearing a peak cap and white arm band; Pigott Thompson is seventh from the left.

Mr Hammond with his Douglas motor cycle *c.* 1912. Note the belt drive, acetylene headlamp, tool box and hand-pump lubrication.

George Batterham, driver of Booth & Fisher's first bus in 1923.

Mrs Hibbard of Park Street Farm at the wheel of her limousine.

D. Simms with an early motor car owned by Mr Collingham. He was employed as a driver of Collingham's charabancs.

Small charabanc outside Bunting's Garage on the De Rhodes crossroads *c*. 1910. The two men at the rear — Davison was killed in the Markham Colliery disaster of 1938 and Jim Smith was seriously injured.

Thirty Clowne ladies aboard the charabanc outside Ottley's premises, probably for an outing to Edwinstowe *c*. 1912.

Mr Stone's charabanc with the Whitwell British Legion Band on board in 1921. The passenger body could be replaced by a haulage body for carrying coal and building materials.

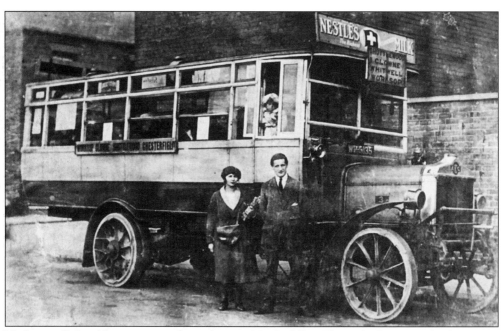

Underwood's local bus service with conductress Mrs Riddley. This vehicle was used in France at the end of the First World War.

The Unity Bus service with conductress Miss Hetty Alcock. In 1927, Ivy Crookes was fined £5 for allowing sixty-two passengers onto a thirty-seater bus — the apprehending policeman stated that their heads looked just like a cart load of turnips!

Clowne National Fire Service fire tender with driver George Gillatt and crew.

Bill Phillips and his two outriders prepare for a spin around Whitwell *c*. 1928. 'Duke' Calladine demonstrates how not to carry a pillion passenger.

CLOWNE SECTION S. C. R. C.

A. SMITH. CLOWNE.

Clowne members of the Sheffield Cyclists Road Club *c*. 1926. Front row, fourth from right, Percy Morris defeated the Great Britain sprint champion over a quarter-mile track race at Lincoln.

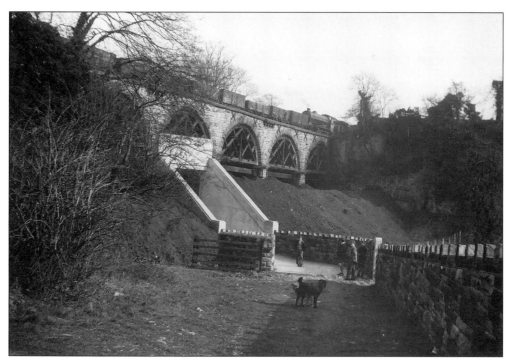

The railway viaduct in Markland Grips prior to demolition.

A passenger train steams into Whitwell Station from Creswell. The first passenger service between Mansfield and Worksop commenced 1 June 1875 and the last passenger train ran on 12 October 1964. The station was dismantled and rebuilt at Butterley, Derbyshire.

Fred Bunting with two members of the LMS staff unload sacks of potatoes in Creswell sidings

Freight waggons passing through Creswell LNER station.

Eight

Ordinary Lives

Men and women sifting for coal to eke out a living. This was a common scene during the miners' strikes of 1912 and 1926.

Barlborough Bellringers in the 1920s with Phillip Hibbard, Mr Kennon and Percy Morris, second, fourth and fifth from the left.

A group of Edwardian 'Elders' in Barlborough. Seated centrally is J.H. Clarkson of Barlborough Electric Co. with A.W. Morris on his left. W.H. Tissington, newsagent, and P. Morris are on the left of the middle row.

Barlborough Section of the North Notts. Association of Bellringers. Rear: R. Reece. P. Morris, H. Hibberd. Front: A. Sturman, P. Hibberd, E. Sturman. The plaque commemorates the ringing of 5,040 changes in three hours on 4 February 1928. The first peal of 'Treble Bob' marked the coming of age of Miss Stella Locker Lampson.

The first council dwelling opened in Barlborough in 1923 was occupied by Mrs Lowe, seen here with her children Arthur, Olive and Frank.

A relaxing afternoon outside the Clowne cricket pavilion *c.* 1890. While the scorer concentrates on the day's play, the reverend gentleman steals forty winks.

J. Denniss, a well-known and popular employee of Eastwood's furniture store which stood opposite to Clowne school.

The end of the road! Children playing with a derelict motor car left behind by gipsy travellers *c*. 1932.

Ted Nixon and his dog. Well known in Clowne as a jack-of-all-trades, he could turn his hand to pig killing, veterinary work and horse shoeing. He worked with a horse and cart, and was also employed on Fielding's farm.

Worthy of the Guiness Book of Records! Albert West holds three wooden bowls in each hand.

George Twining Walker lived at the Manor House Farm, Whitwell. During a weekend shoot he tried to acquire as wide a variety of game as possible. The Canada Goose in his left hand was obtained at the close of the shoot.

James Walter Jones and his Bride Gertrude Keeling at 82 King Street next to Hodthorpe St Martin's Church. Seated are Grandpa' and Grandma' Jones, Minnie Jones and Elias Bowler. The bridesmaids are Ivy and Clarence Jones.

William (Bill) Wardle, popular Hodthorpe miner, councillor, club committee member, pigeon fancier, comedian and entertainer with his wife Edna and daughter Eileen outside No. 14 King Street *c*. 1931.

Whitwell St Lawrence Football Club, winners in 1905 of the Bolton Cup and the Portland Cup.

A group of workers helping at a Clowne Bazaar in 1907.

Mrs Ellis steps carefully onto the Green at Clowne.

A Whitwell Methodist Chapel group *c.* 1860

Whitwell Debating Society *c.* 1910. The society includes the Rector, The Rev. Polehampton and the Parish Constable PC 250.

Hodthorpe Co-operative Women's Guild, 1928. Members include Mesdames Bennett, Bayliss, Towle, Unwin, Crofts, Wasp, Kitts, McCall, Bagshawe, Knowles, Beeston, Butterfield, Turner, Francis, Drury and Yaw. The two girls in white are Esther and Sheila Turner.

Barlborough, Clowne and Whitwell WVS ladies join in a Civil Defence exercise to build a field kitchen. Mrs Presswood is on the extreme left, Mrs Elliot to the right of the chimney with Mrs Lee and Mrs Larner in front of the ovens.

A group of Steetley residents gather outside All Saint's Church for the coronation of Queen Elizabeth II in June 1953.

Whitwell Colliery Cricket Club, cup winners 1946. Standing: B. Olney, Joe Davies, Fred Mellors, Tony Walker, Les Jackson, Dent Webster, George Ward, Percy Jackson. Seated: Colin Womble, Albert Hobson, Maurice Fletcher, Gordon Presgrave, Tom Jones.

Whitwell Welfare Band in the 1930s. Seated in the front row are Mr Ward Walters (fourth) and 'Gaffer' Ellis (sixth), while John Frame is fourth in the middle row.

Whitwell Church Lads Brigade and Junior Corps in camp at Clumber Park, 1927. Owen Evers is fourth right of the junior boys standing on the bench.

Members of the Hodthorpe Soup Kitchen outside the 'tin' chapel *c.* 1920, including Billy Griffin and Mesdames Wasp, Bagshawe, Knowles and Unwin.

The day Whitwell WI went underground, with Ben Owen, Janet Keeton, Eva Lockwood, Delia Wilson, Cath. Biggin, Vi Ellis, Mrs Webster, Florrie Bennett, Ethel Cross, Zoe Hague, Evelyn Mycock, Mrs Boffey, Mrs Ainger, Cyril Chambers, Len Prior and Billy French.

Nine
People at Work

The sinking of Whitwell Colliery shaft on Belph Moor. The first sod was lifted by The Sixth Duke of Portland on Saturday 24 May 1890.

A lump of coal weighing two to three tons and cut from the coal face at Oxcroft No. 3 Colliery for the London Industrial Exhibition.

Maurice Gray handling his pit pony. The last pit ponies were withdrawn from underground work in 1994.

Mr Edwards, winding man at Oxcroft No. 3 Colliery. This was a skilled job, the engine driver holding the lives of hundreds of men in his hands each day and hauling to the surface thousands of tons of coal.

Whitwell Colliery lamp cabin staff behind a notice calling for 'Datallers only on Thursday afternoon' during short-time working c. 1932. Billy Jones is in the centre and Arthur Lomas on the right.

A group of workers at the small dolomite quarry at Steetley in the nineteenth century. The new steelmaking process of the Industrial Revolution and the adjacent steelmaking centre at Sheffield led to the formation of a company in 1885, which was to achieve international renown.

Stone being moved in timber-framed trucks for processing in the cupolas. No personal protective equipment was provided in those days.

All Saints' Church, Steetley, built from the same stone from the quarry as was used for the Houses of Parliament. The building fell into disuse, being used for cock fighting and as a stock pen.

All Saint's Church, Steetley. The building was restored under the guidance of architect R.L. Pearson, RA and reconciled by the Bishop of Lichfield on 2 November 1880.

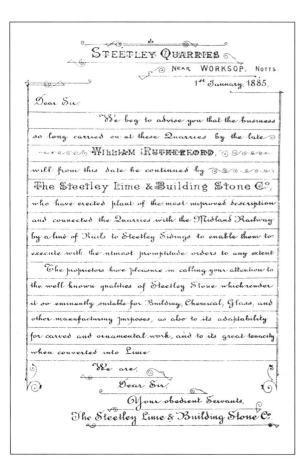

STEETLEY QUARRIES

Near WORKSOP. Notts.

1st January, 1885,

Dear Sir,

We beg to advise you that the business so long carried on at these Quarries by the late WILLIAM RUTHERFORD, will from this date be continued by The Steetley Lime & Building Stone Co., who have erected plant of the most improved description and connected the Quarries with the Midland Railway by a line of Rails to Steetley Sidings to enable them to execute with the utmost promptitude orders to any extent

The proprietors have pleasure in calling your attention to the well known qualities of Steetley Stone which render it so eminently suitable for Building, Chemical, Glass, and other manufacturing purposes, as also to its adaptability for carved and ornamental work, and to its great tenacity when converted into Lime

We are,

Dear Sir,

Your obedient Servants,

The Steetley Lime & Building Stone Co.

Notice of the formation of The Steetley Lime and Building Stone Co. on 1 January 1886 from the private quarry previously operated by John Rutherford.

Laying gas mains at the top of Hangar Hill, Whitwell *c.* 1912.

The water carrier filling up at the village pump in Whitwell before selling around the village at one penny per bucket full.

Tom Taylor, Baker and Confectioner around Clowne and Barlborough *c*. 1910.

Anne Battersby delivering coals in Barlborough *c*. 1880. Each day she drove her horse and cart from Belph and back again, calling at the Portland Arms for ample refreshment at the end of the day, the horse managing to take her home afterwards. She was a descendant of John Battersby who lost his left hand in the Civil War skirmish on Whitwell Common.

A customer leaves the premises of G. Lindley, Saddle and Harness Maker on The Green, Whitwell. The census shows him as a harness maker in 1851.

Mr Lindley's saddlery taken over by Mr Harry Locke with his two sons, Ernest and Harry jnr. Note the stock of army boots, surplus from the First World War.

Stonemasonry was a predominant occupation in the nineteenth century. A local stonemason refurbishes the 'Madonna with Our Lord being carried and John the Baptist being lifted up', which stands in the Lady Chapel of Whitwell Parish Church.

Mr and Mrs Alf Middleton with their first lorry at the launch of their haulage business from 31 Queens Road, Hodthorpe, c. 1921.

Charlie Hunt and his assistant June Wynne park their Co-operative Society milk lorry at the entrance to Hodthorpe during the heavy snowfall of 1979.

The water tower under construction at Barlborough. Water was pumped from Manton Colliery, via Hodthorpe pumping station to storage, then distributed by gravity feed.

Jack Draper on platform duty at the LNER station at Creswell. He also worked as a shunter in the 1930s.

C.W. Geradine was the LNER Stationmaster at Creswell in the 1930s; Douglas Davies was the station clerk.

Men and horses on Creswell pit top ready to take part in a gala day.

Meridian staff on a day's visit to the main works at Beeston to familiarise themselves with the manufacturing equipment following the opening of the factory at Clowne.

Acknowledgements

Compiling a book of photographs like this depends upon the co-operation, generosity, support and trust of numerous people. To those who have helped me I offer my grateful thanks. Most are mentioned by name but there are other friends who have also been supportive, and they will be aware of my deep appreciation.

The collection of photographs for Whitwell was made readily accessible thanks to Malcolm Dolby, George Berry and the Whitwell Library. Creswell and Clowne could have proved more difficult but Roy Fletcher and Albert E. Woodhead, (Damsbrook Drive) made their impressive collections of pictures available. Mrs Olive Watts and Mr & Mrs Walter Morris helped to complete the section on Barlborough.

In finalising the selection many special photographs came to hand, especially from:

Brian Middleton; John & Nancy Wardle; Derek & Eileen Harding;
Tony Walker; Derek & Barbara Wordley; George & Joyce Mallender;
Zoe Hague; Mr & Mrs C.R. Whylde; Tom Simpson,
Rother Valley Transport Society; Redlands Aggregates Limited,
(formerly part of Steetley plc).